FRANCIS OF ASSISI

the Song Goes On

by Hugh Noonan, OFM & Roy M. Gasnick, OFM

D1468693

With ecclesiastical approval
Most Rev. Roger Mahony
Archbishop of Los Angeles, California
February 19, 1987

Editor: Corinne Hart
Design by Bob Miller
Photography: Bill Barrett
Illustrations: Greg Zoltowski, O.F.M.

ISBN-13: 978-0-86716-250-9
ISBN-10: 0-86716-250-3

Published by St. Anthony Messenger Press
28 W. Liberty St.
Cincinnati, OH 45202
www.SAMPBooks.org

Printed in the United States of America.

10 11 12 13 14   12 11 10 9 8 7

This is the story of a great man, a wonderful and simple man. He died over 760 years ago, but he has never been forgotten and he never will be. Great men and women by the thousands have lived and died—kings and queens, conquerors and millionaires, artists, musicians and scholars.

But this man was a roving beggar—a fool for God—and as such, is remembered better than any of the others.

And was loved as none of them was ever loved.

It was not always that way with him. There was a time when his best friends touched their finger to their foreheads in derision when they mentioned his name. Children threw rocks at him. But he had set out on a high adventure, and he kept going.

People stopped laughing.

There was something about the way he touched each person, something about the way he spoke. Birds flew down to perch on his shoulders as he talked, and nature lay quiet under his touch, as it had done for Adam when he walked with God under the trees of Paradise, before the serpent came.

The world stood back in wonder.

This little man had no money but he acted as if he were richer than a millionaire. His body was scarred and racked with pain, but he sang sweeter than any lark. He smiled as he dined with a prince; he laughed as he shared his last crust with a leper. Somehow he had learned to love everything that lived.

And everyone and everything loved him.

He had a secret, a key to God and the universe. The world has been trying to probe that secret ever since.

The Song Begins

The King of Song and Dance

The town of Assisi, set in the hills of Umbria in Italy, looks just the same today as it did in 1181, when Francis Bernardone was born there. His father Pietro was a cloth merchant, married to a gentle lady named Donna Pica. There was at least a second son named Angelo, but Francis was his father's favorite.

Now Pietro Bernardone, by working diligently at his trade, had become rich. He was among the first of the new "middle class," neither noble nor serf. Francis grew up in a house where everything by way of fine clothes, good food, and spending money was his for the asking. The money was soon out of his pockets, for he delighted in giving lavish entertainments for the other young people of Assisi. They ate the choicest food and drank wine that Pietro Bernardone had brought from France, while their host outdid them all in song and hilarity.

Francis knew by heart the verses of the most celebrated troubadours and the dances which came from the Sufis in the Islamic Empire. And afterwards he led the whole company through the streets, pausing beneath dim balconies to serenade the most captivating girls of the town. The people of Assisi dubbed him "King of Song."

Some of the older folk in the town shook

Francis grew up in a house where everything by way of fine clothes, good food, and spending money was his for the asking.

their heads over the future of this lively young man. Others smiled, remembering the bright days of their own youth. Donna Pica was often anxious, and pleaded with her husband not to spoil the boy.But Pietro laughed at her fears, declaring that the only complaint he had against Francis was a habit of wasting good money on beggars.

Pietro Bernardone looked forward to the day when Francis would put his mind to the business of buying and selling cloth. For a time Francis did take his place behind the counter in the shop and so profitably that Pietro was very pleased.

Seeking Glory in War

But Francis unexpectedly, felt only winter in his heart.

There was no lack of wars in those days, when every walled city had its own army. Fighting often broke out between Assisi and the neighboring town of Perugia. So Francis went to war as soon as he was old enough and threw himself into the thick of the battle.

All his high hopes, however, were dashed to the ground, for the Assisians were quickly surrounded and taken prisoner by the Perugians. They led him away in chains to a dungeon, where many of his fellow soldiers sat bemoaning their fate.

Francis could not believe that this was the end for him. He beguiled the other prisoners with the songs of the troubadours and spoke so earnestly of Assisi that they plucked up heart to count off another day. It was a body-draining, spirit-draining year before they were ransomed and allowed to return to Assisi.

Francis as a soldier

Francis got safely back to his father's house. Imprisonment had taken its toll, however. He collapsed on arrival and fell into a feverous coma. Many months passed before he felt strong enough to leave his bed and walk out of the city into the countryside.

It was then spring, of all seasons his favorite, and birds sang in every tree. Flowers carpeted the meadow, and the wind blew sweet.

But Francis, unexpectedly, felt only winter in his heart. These things no longer had the power to stir his heart. Nor did he feel content as before with working in his father's shop, nor in gathering his friends for entertainment and song.

Hardly had Francis recovered to the full when a herald appeared in the streets of Assisi, to announce that the great knight

*Francis!
Who can do
more for you,
the Master or
the servant?*

5

Walter of Brienne was gathering an army to fight for the defense of the Church against the Holy Roman Emperor.

This new, glamorous war triggered Pietro Bernardone's ambitions. He was a prosperous merchant, but that was as high on the social ladder as he could go. He began to scheme how his son might find glory in the war and thus enter the ranks of the nobility, to become **Sir** Francis Bernardone.

His son rolled the title on his tongue and liked it very well. He began to dream of common folk bowing as "Sir Francis" rode by with a band of armed men at his heels, carrying shields and banners emblazoned with his coat of arms. A castle would be his, and servants and farms with tenants. Then marriage with a noble lady as good as she was beautiful.

But first the son of the cloth merchant must be knighted, and this could be done most easily on the battlefield, after he had fought with valor in the service of a great lord.

The night before Francis rode off to battle he had a dream, and in this dream he saw himself in a vast hall. The walls were lined with swords, shields and banners, trophies of a victorious army. A voice said to Francis, "All these shall belong to you and your followers."

Francis was ready for his second war. His father gave him a warhorse of matchless spirit and a suit of armor whose breastplate was inlaid with gold.

He had galloped only a mile or so along the road when he met a knight who was also on his way to join the army of Walter of Brienne. This knight had returned recently

Francis knew this Assisi street as a wild youth and as a saint

from the wars against the Moslems in the Holy Land. During his absence, his own property had suffered neglect, and he was reduced to such poverty that he had to go about in battered armor on a rack-of-bones horse.

As Francis rode along beside this knight, he began to feel ashamed of being mounted on a charger and wearing new armor, while a man who carried the Crusaders' Cross appeared in this sorry state. So he gave the knight his own horse and equipment.

That same evening, weary from his ride, Francis lay in his tent. Suddenly, from the deepest part of his heart, he heard a voice call his name: "Francis! Who can do more for you, the Master or the servant"?

There was a gentleness in these words that gave Francis courage to answer, "The Master." "Why, then," asked the voice, "do you follow the servant instead of the Master?" Francis somehow knew it was God who spoke to him. He cried out, "Lord, what do you want me to do?" The voice said, "Return home. You have misunderstood the former vision. It will have a different fulfillment."

In the morning, Francis left the army. It was hard to face the questioning, the taunts of desertion, the suggestions of cowardice, the disgrace in the eyes of his father. Yet he told no one of his vision. He went back to helping his father sell bolts of cloth and to playing King of Song for his friends. But nothing that he did pleased him as it formerly had.

Francis . . . prayed with all his heart and soul that God might unlock for him the mystery behind his confusion.

The Caves

Francis began to go out often to caves and secret places in the woods, and to pray with all his heart and soul that God might unlock for him the mystery behind his confusion.

He prayed for the "voice" to speak again, to instruct him. No voice spoke. Doubts troubled him. Had he really heard God's voice? Or was it his own? Was he going insane? When he thought of his past folly, he grew afraid that he was all unworthy to speak to God, much less to serve Him.

Then he thought of God's mercy and he was comforted. A sense of peace began slowly to pervade his soul. Winter lost its grip on his heart, opening the way for spring. Marvelous, daring, dramatic thoughts filled his mind.

The solitude, the prayer, the facing of self in the cave experience had done their job.

The solitude, the prayer, the facing of self in the cave experience had done their job. The failed **Sir** Francis was now ready to become **Brother** Francis.

Francis Finds His Lady

Soon after these cave experiences, Francis was again leading his friends through the streets of Assisi. At one point, the group noticed that Francis had disappeared. They went back a little, until they found him standing like a man in a trance. One of them cried, "Francis is in love!" And Francis answered, "Yes, I am! But the bride I am going to win is nobler, richer and fairer than any woman you know!"

His friends all laughed, which they would

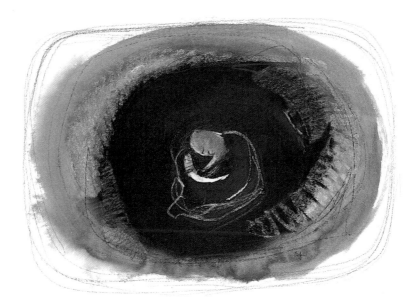

Francis in solitude

not have done had they known that Francis would never again reign as king of their revels, nor lead them carelessly in singing through the night.

For in that street beneath the stars, he had been suddenly entranced by the love of God.

In that night he had caught the first glimmering of the secret which was to be his and which he was to give the world.

He was to find joy not in **having** but in **giving.**

He would strip himself of all the things of this world which might turn his heart away from God. Through poverty of body he would be satisfied with the simplest of food and clothing. Through poverty of soul he would give up all desires except one—to do the will of God. He had found freedom.

He gave a name to that freedom, a name

He was to find joy not in having but in giving.

9

which blended the language of the trou-
badors and the language of the caves: Lady
Poverty.

The Leper

Francis now found himself giving more
freely than ever to beggars, as well as
seeking out the sick so that he could
give even more of himself. He drew the line
at lepers, however. In the past, he could
never bring himself to approach a leper,
although he often threw them coins from a
distance. Then, one day, as he was riding
his horse in the valley below Assisi, he saw
directly in his path a beggar ravaged by
leprosy. Francis first turned away. Then in
shame at this treatment of a new-found
brother in Christ, he dismounted and drew
near the leper. He placed a coin in the
bleeding hand. And then he kissed the
leper.

. . . he would give up all desires except one — to do the will of God. He had found freedom.

In sudden joy of soul, he remounted for
his ride. With the Lord's help, he had won a
great victory over himself.

It turned out to be the pivotal victory of
his life.

Later, he was to write in his *Testament:*
"The Lord granted me, Brother Francis, to
begin to do penance in this way: while I was
in sin, it seemed very bitter to me to see
lepers. But the Lord himself led me among
them and I had mercy upon them. When I
left them, that which seemed bitter to me
was changed into sweetness of soul and

*(Photo left)
The tunic of Francis
preserved in the
Basilica in Assisi*

11

body. Afterward, I lingered a little and then left the world."

Another part of Francis' secret: God reveals himself so often in people we don't want to like.

Rebuild My House

One of his favorite places of prayer was the abandoned chapel of San Damiano, one of the many which stood in the valley below Assisi. On most of these the roofs gaped and the walls crumbled with neglect. There was an exposed Byzantine style crucifix before which Francis liked especially to pray.

One day while he was kneeling before this sign of the Lord's love for his people, the "voice" of the Lord spoke to him again: "Francis, go and rebuild my house, which is falling into ruins."

God reveals himself so often in people we don't like.

Now, the only houses of the Lord which Francis knew were the churches. He looked around at San Damiano. Here at last was something for him to do. Like the careful businessman his father had taught him to be, he first figured up the cost of roof, walls and furnishings. Then he leaped onto his horse and galloped into Assisi and to his father's shop.

Pietro Bernardone was away on one of his trips so without question from anyone, Francis snatched up rolls of the finest cloth and raced off with it to the market town of Foligno. He quickly found a buyer for the material. Just in case he might need more money, he sold the horse as well. Then as quickly as he could, he made his way on foot to San Damiano.

An old priest, poor but generous, was

Francis hears the call.

living at the chapel. Into his hands, Francis poured out the money from his sale of the cloth and the horse, asking the priest to use it for stone and mortar and furnishing of the chapel. The priest, however, shrank from the gold for fear of Pietro Bernardone.

But he did allow Francis to live with him at San Damiano. In Francis' mind, he had now "left the world." Though the notion was as yet still vague, he somehow knew that he had become a "servant of God."

He shivered in that windy shelter. Pinched with cold and hunger, he thought of his father's house with its laden table and warm beds. Still, in doing the will of God, his heart sang with a joy he had never dreamed of when he sat with a cup of wine before a fire. So for the love of God he commanded his body to do the pleasure of his soul.

Francis, go and rebuild my house, which is falling into ruins.

13

The Crazy Man

Pietro Bernardone returned finally from France, where he had been traveling. He had no sooner set foot in the town than he heard talk of what Francis had done with the cloth and the horse. He cried first, "My son!" and then "My gold!"

He went straight to San Damiano. Francis, forewarned of his father's coming, hid himself in a secret place which he had prepared for such an emergency. After hiding for a month in this refuge, Francis learned to put his trust in the Lord. He called himself a coward and no true knight of Christ because up to this time he had been afraid to face his father or any of his old friends in Assisi.

He took the path which led through the woods to the town. As he passed along the streets, all the people who saw him stopped to stare. They were accustomed to seeing Francis Bernardone dressed in the height of fashion, and now he appeared with his garments soiled and torn, and his face ghostly with fasting.

His old friends were ashamed, and looked quickly away. But the serfs began to follow him, laughing and crying out, "Look at the crazy man!" And they pelted him with stones and trash. The children also joined in the mockery.

Pietro Bernardone was in his shop. The shouting of the crowd drew him to the door. What he saw burned the eyes in his head—his favorite son, his heir, covered with mud and followed by a jeering rabble. Maddened by this blow to his pride, he pulled Francis into the shop, loaded him

The chapel of San Damiano where Francis received his vocation. Later, it became the first residence of the Poor Clares.

with blows and curses, and afterwards locked him in a cellar room. Then to escape wagging tongues, he set off on another journey.

No sooner had Pietro Bernardone left the house than Francis' mother, Donna Pica, unlocked the cellar door and went to her son. She found him nursing his bruises with good cheer. She could not understand all that he said to her then, but one thing was clear in her mind. Francis believed his new way of life was God's will, and therefore neither she nor his father had a right to stand in his way.

She brought him good food, and made him eat it, and put more in his pockets to take with him. Then she gave him her blessing and surrendered him to God. So Francis returned to San Damiano.

Plea for Enlightenment

So for the love of God he commanded his body to do the pleasure of his soul.

How had Francis, the former golden boy of Assisi, been able to stand up to all that derision? Because he tenaciously hung onto another secret he had discovered in the caves: prayer.

The prayer he offered over and over again is one his followers have come to call the "prayer for enlightenment:"

*Most high,
glorious God,
enlighten the darkness of my heart
and give me, Lord,
a correct faith,
a certain hope,
a perfect charity,
sense and knowledge,
so that I may carry out Your holy
and true command.*

A Father Lost and One Found

When Pietro Bernardone came back and missed Francis from the cellar, he found no words hard enough for his son. He called his lawyers and ordered them to draw up papers to bring Francis to court. Pietro would either break the boy's will or cut him off from family, goods and property. This trial had to be held before the Bishop of Assisi because Francis had declared himself a servant of God. On the day of the hearing, all the people of Assisi showed up in the cathedral square.

So, dressed again in his fine clothes, Francis faced his father in the presence of the Bishop and all the people. The Bishop said to Francis: "Even if you wish to serve the Church, you have no right under pretence of good works to keep money that you may have obtained unjustly. Give this money back to your father, to quiet him."

Then Francis said to the Bishop, "My Lord, I will not only give him the money cheerfully, but also the clothes I have received from him."

He stripped off his scarlet cloak and his suit of fine material, and stood naked before the crowd. He cried out: "Listen, all of you! Up to now I have called Pietro Bernardone 'father.' Now I return to him his money and all the clothes I have received from him, so that from now on I shall say not 'Father Pietro Bernardone,' but 'Our Father in Heaven'."

He laid both clothes and money at Pietro Bernardone's feet. The father was first

For now his life rested entirely in the hands of his Father in heaven.

*Francis renounces
his earthly father.*

struck dumb with amazement; then with his face set like stone, he picked up both clothes and money and left the court.

Then the Bishop wrapped his own cloak around Francis' shoulders, until another was brought by the gardener, an old one which he found in a closet. Francis, after he had put on this poor cloak, walked out of the square and through the gates of Assisi into the countryside.

As he went he sang. For now his life rested entirely in the hands of his Father in heaven. Lady Poverty had set him free, free from money, free from the desire for power, free from hindering family ties. So he wandered, trusting and joyful as the forest birds who live from the storehouse of God.

Then Francis returned to San Damiano and to his work of rebuilding chapels.

He no longer had money to buy stone for

Lady Poverty had set him free.

the walls. So he went with a basket from door to door, calling, "He who gives one stone, will receive one blessing; for two stones, two blessings; three stones, three blessings!" He received more scorn than stones. He accepted both with a cheerful face, glad to suffer even derision in his newfound service of the Lord.

When San Damiano was finished, he rebuilt other chapels in this same way.

Francis "Discovers" the Gospel

It was at one such small church, popularly called The Portiuncula, or Little Portion, that another turning point came in Francis' life. He loved this particular church above the others because it was dedicated to *Santa Maria de Los Angeles* (a name his followers later gave to what has become the U.S.'s second largest city).

While attending Mass there one day, he heard these words read from the Gospel of St. Matthew:

This is what I want, this is what I seek, this is what I long for with all my inmost heart.

> Go, preach the message. "The kingdom of heaven is at hand!" Cure the sick, raise the dead, cleanse the lepers, cast out devils. Freely you have received, freely give. Do not keep gold, or silver, or money in your purses, no wallet for your journey, nor two tunics, nor sandals, nor staff; for the laborer deserves his living. And whatever town or village you

(Photo left)
The Basilica of the Portiuncula enshrines the original chapel

Francis the joyful beggar

enter, inquire who in it is worthy, and stay there until you leave. As you enter the house, salute it, saying, "Peace to this house."

When Francis heard these words, a cry came out from his deepest soul, "This is what I want, this is what I seek, this is what I long for with all my inmost heart!" He took off his shoes and went with bare feet. He exchanged his simple robe for the rough tunic of a peasant, which he gathered about the waist with a piece of frayed rope.

When he had done this, the Lord gave him to understand that he was not called to restore chapels but to rebuild the Church of God throughout the world. He wasted not a minute in starting this work but went straight to the market place.

Not followers, not disciples, not subjects— but brothers.

In gathering a crowd he had no trouble at all, for the buyers and sellers alike left the stalls to come and laugh at him. But he faced them all with a smile, and he greeted them, "May the Lord give you peace!" Then be began to speak to them from his heart of the love and the goodness of God. And they hushed each other to silence. He was not preaching in Latin. He used Italian, the new language of the people. He spoke simply and beautifully about things that really mattered to them. And they were stirred to their souls.

Then Francis took a final step for his Lady Poverty. He took up a bowl and began to beg his food every day from door to door.

"The Lord Gave Me Some Brothers"

One of the most touching sentiments Francis ever wrote was the words, "And the Lord gave me some brothers." Not followers, not disciples, not subjects—but brothers.

The first was Bernard of Quintavalle, a young man of position and wealth in Assisi. For many years, Bernard had been looking for a way to come closer to God. He marveled at how exactly this man's deeds matched his words.

Bernard invited Francis to stay at his house, and in the night, when they were in the same room, Bernard made believe that he was fast asleep. Then Francis rose from his bed and knelt to pray. The whole night Bernard watched him secretly, and Francis said only this one prayer, "My God and my All! My God and my All!"

At first Bernard thought him a stupid person to be saying these words all night long. Then he asked himself what more need one say, if these words were meant from one's heart. He knew that here was the one who would lead him closer to God.

Shortly after that, a lawyer named Peter came to Francis for the same purpose, then a peasant by the name of Giles.

The four of them went about the country-side, living on God's bounty as freely as the birds. They worked for their daily bread, begging only when no work came to hand. They shared both crust and cup with the hungry, and when they had given away everything except the clothes that covered them, they tore off sleeves or hoods and

The home of Francis' first follower, Bernard of Quintavalle

gave the cloth to the poor to sell. They preached to the people everywhere, on the roads and in the market places. And they cared for lepers and other outcasts, as Francis believed the Gospel directed.

In all things they followed the example of Francis. He looked after their health with care, and ordered them to take the food and sleep which each needed to serve the Lord. None was to envy those who could work on a crust, nor look down on those who needed half a loaf. On one occasion, when Francis realized that a sick brother would benefit from some extra food but was too ashamed to ask for it, Francis took him into an arbor and sat down to eat with him so that no one might point a finger at the brother.

. . . the Church needed reform . . . the Gospel message of loving service had become blurred.

If Francis abhorred the idea of "big brother is watching you," he relished the idea of being a "little brother."

The Reluctant Pope

When the number of brothers who followed Francis had come to eleven, he made up his mind to go to Rome and ask the approval of the Pope for this way of life.

So all twelve went to Rome. Francis talked first with some Cardinals, but all of them except for one shook their heads at the thought that any group of men could live the Gospel literally, without property or possessions of their own.

There were scores of fiery reformers, mostly heretics, scouring Europe at the time, demanding reforms in the Church. And the Church needed reform. It had become so rich, so mighty, so concerned

The first followers

with civil power that the Gospel message of loving service had become blurred.

Indeed, when Francis appeared before Pope Innocent III, the most powerful man in the world, the Pope dismissed him harshly. But that night the Pope had a dream. He saw the vast Church of St. John Lateran begin to lean and to fall. This church was the Vatican of its day, the seat of all Christianity. The Pope understood that the whole structure of the Church was ready to collapse. Then he saw a small man in a ragged garment. Tiny as an ant before the gigantic building, the man, nevertheless, laid his shoulder against a wall and pushed the church back into place.

Slowly, he turned his head toward the Pope and Innocent III saw that the man was Francis.

The very next day the Pope approved

At the heart of Francis' visionary way of life stood the Gospel . . . a burning message of love.

ΕΓΩ ΕΙΜΙ ΤΟ ΦΩΣ
ΤΟΥ ΚΟΣΜΟΥ Ο Α
ΚΟΛΟΥΘΩΝ ΕΜΟΙ
ΟΥ ΜΗ ΠΕΡΙΠΑΤΗΣ
ΗΕΝ ΤΗ ΣΚΟΤΙΑ ΑΛΛ
ΕΞΕΙ ΤΟ ΦΩΣ ΤΗΣ ΖΩΗΣ

EGO SUM LUX MUNDI QUI
SEQUITUR ME NON
AMBULAT IN TENEBRIS
SET ABEBIT LUME
VITE †

ΙΗΡ ΧΝ ΟΑ ΟΥ ΓΑΒΡΙΗΛ

the way of life Francis had described:

The rule and life of the lesser brothers is this: to observe the holy Gospel of our Lord Jesus Christ, by living in obedience, without anything of their own, and in chastity.

At the heart of Francis' visionary way of life stood the Gospel, not as intellectualized by the scholastics of the day, but as a burning message of love, compassion, forgiveness, reconciliation and peace.

His followers were not to be considered as "soldiers of Christ," but as brothers, real brothers, whose interests were not in wealth and power but in the saving grace of helping the poor, oppressed, and spiritually wounded peoples of this earth.

The Lord Gives Francis Sisters

His followers . . . interests were in the saving grace of helping the poor, oppressed, and spiritually wounded people of this earth.

Now that Francis had approval from the Pope, he preached in churches. One day he mounted the pulpit in the Cathedral of San Rufino in Assisi. Among the crowd stood a young lady of noble family, Clare Favarone.

Every word that Francis spoke of the joys of poverty and the total service of the Lord found an echo in her heart. For many years she had yearned to spend her life for God, but her family urged her constantly to marry.

(Photo left)
"Christ, the Judge,"
a common representation
of Jesus at the time
of Francis

After Clare had listened to Francis, she went to visit him in the company of relatives who understood her heart. Francis, after talking with her several times, discovered that she had both courage and strength of will. So, in spite of fierce opposition from her family, he allowed her to come one night with a relative to San Damiano. Here Francis cut the hair from her head and covered her with the veil of a nun. Francis knew that other young women would come to join her so he gave her San Damiano for her convent.

Shortly after, Clare's own sister Agnes came, and eventually another sister, Beatrice, and even their mother Ortolana. They spent their days in prayer and in caring for the sick who were brought to them. They walked barefoot and wore rough habits like Francis and his brothers. They owned no property and took no money, but ate bread which was given to them by the people out of charity. Many other women came to the Convent of San Damiano, and Clare taught them to serve the Lord with joy.

At first they were called the Poor Ladies; now they are known as the Poor Clares.

Every word that Francis spoke of the joys of poverty and the total service of the Lord found an echo in her heart.

The Family Expands

When people all over the countryside heard Francis speak with such fire of the love and compassion of Christ, they too wanted to share in Francis' vision and mission.

They came and begged Francis to give them a rule of peace like those he had made for the brothers and for the Poor Clares. So Francis set down for these people "in the

Francis and Clare

world" a way of life which came to be called at first the Order of Penance, then the Third Order, and now, the Secular Franciscans.

In the spirit of his Lady Poverty, he begged them to be plain and simple in food and dress and to share what they saved in this manner with the poor. They were never to commit any sinful action for the sake of profit or power over other people. And they were to establish the peace of Christ by refusing to bear arms or take the oath of fealty.

People by the thousands, with their spouses and their families, hurried to accept this Rule. They shared cheerfully with all those in need, the sick, the poor, and the oppressed.

In those times, the great lords could send their subjects into bloody wars for any

. . . they too wanted to share in Francis' vision and mission.

petty question of pride or ownership of a scrap of land. But now men by the thousands had pledged themselves not to take up the sword. Many a lord was hardpressed to raise an army. Francis had done something concrete to bring about the peace of Christ: he had set in motion the downfall of the feudal system.

The Word Goes Out

Francis himself was so eager to preach his newly-discovered Gospel of peace and reconciliation that he immediately sent his brothers out in groups, first to the other countries of Europe and then to the Islamic-controlled territories of Africa.

He decided for himself to go to the Holy Land, even though it was occupied by the hostile Islamic forces. Joining one of the Crusades to free the Holy Land, he landed in Egypt only to find, to his horror, that the Christian Crusaders were as evil and immoral as he had judged the Moslems to be.

Francis, who once had played at war, now saw the futility of all war.

Francis, who once had played at war, now saw the futility of all war. He took matters—and his life—into his own hands and with a companion made off into the desert to find the Sultan.

The Sultan's soldiers found them first and almost killed them, until their leader realized these were men the Sultan might want to meet.

So Francis came face to face with the supposed anti-Christ himself, Al-Malik al-Kamil. What he found amazed him: the Sultan, in his own right, was a religious man. The two became friends.

30

"Become a Christian," Francis said to the Sultan, "and the war between us will cease."

"If all Christians were as you, the Sultan replied, there would be no war between us."

Francis left sad because he could not stop the war but happy because he achieved what the Crusaders did not: free passage to the Holy Land.

Trouble

Francis returned from the mid-East with a permanent eye disease and other illnesses resulting from his overly severe self-denials. His physical troubles were matched by problems he found in his brotherhood.

Just twelve years earlier, there had been only the original group of twelve. Now there were more than 5,000. Few had met Francis personally. The fervor and desires of the rest were not equal to that of Francis.

The Pope told Francis that the brotherhood needed more organization, new rules, greater control if it were to survive. Angered at first, Francis finally saw the wisdom of the Pope's message.

Sick in heart, he resigned as head of the brotherhood. Confused in heart, he wondered if God had abandoned him and his dream. As he did in his youth, he retreated to the caves—to pray, to find perspective, to plan with God the rest of the life allotted to him.

The San Damiano Crucifix, now housed in the Basilica of St. Clare

A New Birth

In the caves, Francis discovered how much God was with him still. "My brothers," he said to his closest friends, "let us begin again, for up to now we have done nothing."

That winter he had an inspiration. He recalled how much the story of Christmas had influenced him not to become a cloistered monk, but rather to go out into the market place, where the people are. Now he wanted people themselves to know that God was truly here among them.

He arranged for a special drama on Christmas night in the town of Greccio, where he had been staying. In a cave in the hills, there would be a "Mary and Joseph," an ox and an ass, and a midnight Mass to bring Jesus on earth again. He taught the townspeople special hymns and then led them to the cave. The people were overwhelmed. They could "see" with their own eyes the meaning of Incarnation.

Historians like to point out that here, at Greccio, was the origin of the Christmas crib, Christmas carols, and Renaissance drama.

Let us begin again, for up to now we have done nothing.

God's Seal of Approval

There is a mountain north of Assisi called La Verna. A wealthy man who owned this property gave it to Francis for a place of prayer. Here in September of the year 1224, he went to keep the fast before the feast of St. Michael the Archangel. He made a shelter for himself among the rocks, in a cave that had been the home of a beast.

The crib at Greccio

When it was the 14th day of September, which is the feast of the Holy Cross, he stood on a ledge of rock that stretched outside this cave. And he prayed:

O Lord Jesus Christ,
I beg you
to give me two graces
before I die.
First, that in my lifetime
I may feel in body and soul
as far as possible
the pain you endured
in the hour of
your most bitter sufferings.
Second, that I may feel
in my heart
as far as possible
that excess of love
by which you,
O Son of God,

He wanted people to know that God was truly here among them.

33

were inflamed to
undertake so cruel
a suffering
for us sinners.

When he finished this prayer, a brightness lit the sky. Francis saw coming toward him with the swiftness of an arrow a figure of Christ Crucified. Francis who had tried all his days to become like Christ in body and in heart found that God himself had finished this work.

For now there appeared in Francis' hands, feet and side, wounds that bled and burned like those which Christ bore upon the Cross.

Canticle of the Sun

From that hour, Francis hid his feet with sandals and lowered his sleeves over his hands. But no amount of caution kept the people from discovering one way or another that he had been fashioned into a living image of Christ.

By this time, Francis was so worn with pain and sickness that he had to ride a little donkey. At every village to which word of his coming spread, all the men and the women, young and old, came out to meet him. They knelt along the roadway, and as he passed, they reached to touch his sandal or the edge of his sleeve, or even the bridle of the donkey.

He begged them often not to do these things, but more often when he rode through villages he saw neither houses nor

Francis who had tried all his days to become like Christ in body and in heart found that God himself had finished this work.

(Photo left)
The wounds of the crucified Christ in Francis' hands

people. For his body and his soul were taken up entirely with the memory of that face of Christ which had looked at him with love and pain in his vision of the Crucified on Mount La Verna.

His body now was like an over-driven donkey and could not be made to rise again. So Francis had to lie still and let himself be cared for and doctored.

It was at this time that he composed new praises of God which he called the *Canticle of Brother Sun*, a song which soars to heaven with the swiftness of the lark:

No amount of caution kept the people from discovering one way or another that he had been fashioned into a living image of Christ.

Most High, all-powerful, good Lord,
Yours are the praises, the glory, the
honor, and all blessing.
To You alone, Most High, do they
belong,
and no man is worthy to mention
Your name.
Praised be You, my Lord, with all
Your creatures,
especially Sir Brother Sun,
who is the day and through whom
You give us light.
And he is beautiful and radiant with
great splendor;
and bears a likeness of You, Most
High One.
Praised be You, my Lord, through
Sister Moon and the stars,
in heaven You formed them clear and
precious and beautiful.
Praised be You, my Lord, through
Brother Wind,
and through the air, cloudy and
serene, and every kind of weather
through which You give sustenance
to Your creatures.

Canticle of
Brother Sun

Praised be You, my Lord, through
    Sister Water,
which is very useful and humble and
    precious and chaste.
Praised be You, my Lord, through
    Brother Fire,
through whom You light the night
and he is beautiful and playful and
    robust and strong.
Praised be You, my Lord, through
    our Sister Mother Earth,
who sustains and governs us,
and who produces varied fruits with
    colored flowers and herbs.
Praised be You, my Lord, through
    those who give pardon for
Your love
and bear infirmity and tribulation.
Blessed are those who endure in
    peace

**. . . all the men
and women,
young and old,
came to meet
him.**

37

for by You, Most High, they shall be
crowned.
Praised be You, my Lord, through
our Sister Bodily Death,
from whom no living man can escape.
Woe to those who die in mortal sin.
Blessed are those whom death will
find in Your most holy will,
for the second death shall do them
no harm.
Praise and bless my Lord and give
Him thanks and serve Him with
great humility.

Into Eternity Singing

. . . his body and his soul were taken up entirely with the memory of that face of Christ which had looked at him with love and pain . . .

In spite of all doctoring and care, Francis felt the one he called Sister Death approach nearer every day. He begged his brothers to carry him home again to the Portiuncula.

When they came to a hill outside the walls of Assisi, he asked them to place him in such a way that he faced the city. Then he blessed the town of his birth, its houses, walls and streets where he had walked with his dreams and found the joy of their fulfillment. And after that, they carried Francis to the Portiuncula.

In the last few weeks of September of 1226, he waited, spending his days begging his brothers in word and in writing to be faithful to the holy Gospel. And while his body wasted away, his soul burned with a joy that warmed everyone who came near him.

On the first day of October, he heard Sister Death at the door. He asked to be stripped of his habit and to be laid on the bare ground so that he might die with nothing, as Christ had upon the Cross. But the brother guardian ordered him to accept the habit which another brother gave him.

Francis was glad to take this as a gift to a poor man. Then he raised his hand in a blessing for all his brothers, those who stood near, those who were in far places, and those who were yet to come down through the years: "I have done what was mine to do. May Christ now teach you yours." On Saturday, the third day of October, with the day darkening into twilight, Francis welcomed Sister Death into his presence.

His brothers knelt beside him, trying with prayer to hold back the sobs and watching him by the light of a little candle. They saw his face grow bright with joy. Then he began to sing with them the 141st Psalm down to the words, "Lead my soul out of prison." The brothers finished the last words all alone.

Francis of Assisi had entered heaven, singing.

His Song Goes On

He left this world having touched this world as few before—or since—have had the power to do. Even in his own lifetime, people puzzled about his secret, his ability to touch someone or something and produce a change for the better.

The tomb of
St. Francis

"Why after you, why after you?" asked one of the brothers, half-teasingly, during the height of Francis' fame. "Why does all the world seem to be running after you to see you, hear you and obey you? You are not a handsome man. You do not have great learning or wisdom. You are not a nobleman. So why after you?"

Francis loved the teasing, but his answer was straightforward. "Why after me? I have this from the All-Holy himself. His eyes roamed the earth and could not find one creature more insufficient, more foolish, more vile than myself. So, to do that wonderful work he intends to do in this world, he chose me so that everyone would know that it is God at work here and not Francis Bernardone."

Another answer, perhaps even closer to the truth, is offered by Ernest Raymond: "He preached by his life, which is the best way, the most effective Christian sermon that has ever been preached; a sermon that still, after all the centuries, works its gentle ferment and attains its design, because if in reading it we learn to love Francis, we must find ourselves loving also his Master and his Model."

In spite of all doctoring and care Francis felt the one he called Sister Death approach nearer every day.

And so, his song goes on. In Assisi, San Francisco, Los Angeles, Tokyo, Manila, Nairobi, Sydney, and other places he never dreamed of. In the artists and poets who glorify him as a human ideal. In the writers and historians who view his values as essential for survival today. In the peace-makers who take heart from his heart. In the environmentalists who carry on his respect for animals and nature. In the social activists who know now that one person can make a difference. In the Franciscan Orders, male and female, clerical and lay, Catholic and Protestant. In the hearts of all who wrestle with God.

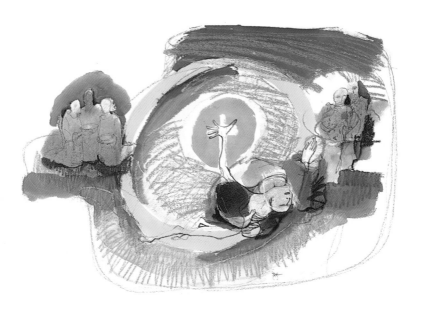

Francis and
Sister Death

**I have done
what was mine
to do.
May Christ
now teach
you yours.**